Mastering Table Topics

Second Edition

By Matthew Arnold Stern

Matthew Arnold Stern
Lake Forest, California
www.matthewarnoldstern.com
Twitter: @maswriter

Copyright © 2012–2015, Matthew Arnold Stern. All rights reserved.

Printed in the United States of America. No part of this publication may be reproduced in any form without the written permission of the author, except by a reviewer who wishes to quote brief passages in connection with a review written for inclusion in a magazine, newspaper, or broadcast.

To view Matthew Arnold Stern's other writing, including speeches, essays, and communication tips, visit his Web site at www.matthewarnoldstern.com.

Second edition, September 2015

ISBN: 978-1-329-46495-7

Cover image by Bigstock (photo ID 48723890) www.bigstockphoto.com

Contents

Introduction 1
How this Book Can Help You 2
Table Topics Are Fun! 2

How to Run Table Topics 3
Topicmaster 3
Table Topic Questions 3
Timekeeper and Timing Equipment 4
Vote Counter, Voting Ballots, and Awards 5

How to Answer Table Topic Questions 7
Step 1: Understand the Question 7
   Listen Carefully 7
   Wait 7
   Listen to Background Information 8
   Ask Again and for Clarification 8
Step 2: Select What You Are Going to Cover 9
Step 3: Organize Your Thoughts 9
   Importance of Organization 10
   General Rule for Organization 10
   Applying Organization to Table Topics 11
   Opening 11
   Body 11
   Conclusion 12
   How to Organize Your Speech Quickly 12
Step 4: Deliver Your Speech 12
   Eye Contact 13
   Vocal Variety 13
   Body Language 14
   Additional Tips 14
Examples 14

Workplace Questions 19
If I Were in Charge 21
Interview Questions 22
Spin Doctors 23
Status Report 25

  Convince Me... *26*
  Bad Ideas.. *28*
  Recovery.. *30*
  Dealing with Hostility..................................... *31*
  Global Business... *33*
  Executive Decision... *34*
  Breaking the News... *36*
  Career Choices.. *38*

Special Seasons and Events Questions............... **39**
  Happy New Year!.. *41*
  Winter Questions.. *42*
  Isn't It Romantic?.. *43*
  Spring.. *44*
  Mother's and Father's Days............................ *45*
  Graduation.. *46*
  Summer... *48*
  The Post-September 11 World........................ *49*
  It's Spooky... *50*
  Trick or Treat!.. *51*
  Holiday Shopping... *52*
  Secret Santa.. *53*

Thoughts and Feelings Questions......................... **55**
  Personal Values.. *57*
  Courage... *58*
  Turning Points.. *59*
  That Makes Me So Mad!.................................. *60*
  Opposing View... *61*
  Get Happy!... *62*
  What Do You Think Of..................................... *63*
  Life Stages... *64*
  What Do You Do?.. *65*
  Making Changes... *66*
  Big Issues... *67*

Potpourri Questions... **69**
  Finish This.. *71*
  The Language of Flowers................................ *73*
  Dogs.. *74*
  Cats... *75*
  How Do I?... *76*

#masteringtabletopics Questions *77*
Let's Go to the Movies! *78*
Think Fast! *79*
Fear Factor *80*
What If? *81*
Free Advice *83*
Why? *84*
Eighties Retro *85*
The Last Forty Years *86*
A Mile in Your Shoes *87*
Speech Contest Questions *88*

Other Ideas for Table Topics **89**

How to Develop Your Own Questions **91**

Additional Resources **93**
   Books and Games *93*
      The Book of Questions Series *93*
      TableTalk *93*
      TableTopics *93*
   Apps for Table Topics *93*
      Timing Apps *93*
      Table Topic Question Apps *94*

Index **95**

Introduction

"Why do you think you're qualified for this position?"

"What is your opinion about the proposal?"

"Mommy, why can't I wear that outfit to school!?"

Every day, we are confronted with questions. And every day, we have to come up with answers.

Table topics can prepare you to answer these questions. You are given a topic to speak about, and you come up with a brief, well-organized impromptu talk of one to two minutes in length.

Sounds easy? Like checkers or bike riding, table topics is easy to learn, but requires dedicated practice to master. There are several skills that you will develop.

The first skill is just getting up to speak. We have all heard the statistic that most people fear public speaking more than death. This is no exaggeration. Toastmasters club generally give guests the option to participate in table topics. I have known people who have declined for weeks until they mustered up the courage to take a question. One woman passed on table topics questions for six weeks. After she took her first question, she became comfortable enough to get up and speak. She then started giving speeches and became an active member. After a few years, she became the club's president. As you gain experience in speaking, you too will overcome your fears and become more proficient.

The second skill is answering questions. We appreciate straight answers. We get enough obfuscation and double-speak from bosses, politicians, and media personalities. Table topics help you practice understanding questions so that you can give appropriate answers. Listening is as important to table topics as speaking.

The third skill is organization. How do you present your ideas so that your listener feels moved to act on them? In table topics, you learn how to give an opening that gets your listener's attention, develop a body of points that flow logically, and conclude so that your main idea stays in the listener's mind.

The final skill is brevity. One to two minutes does not give you much time to speak (although most people consider their first table topic to be the longest minute of their lives). In many situations, one to two minutes is all the time you have to get your idea across – such as when you are giving a sales pitch to a busy executive, when you are invited to speak on television, or when you meet a prospective client at a busy conference. You have to learn to get your idea across in a short period of time – and encourage that listener to grant you more time to speak.

The more you participate in table topics, the more complete and better organized your answers will be and the more confident you will feel in speaking. As you refine your skills in table topics, you will feel more comfortable in handling other speaking situations.

How this Book Can Help You

To make the most out of a workout, you need the proper exercise equipment and a qualified trainer. The same is true with table topics. You need quality questions that challenge and stimulate you and encourage you to come up with a great response.

The book contains table topics questions that I have presented at Toastmasters clubs and other organizations over the years. Included are questions for a variety of subjects, including business, special times of the year, thoughts and feelings, and even how to give instructions.

This book also provides tips for answering table topic questions. Learn how to listen to questions, answer directly, and organize your talk.

Table Topics Are Fun!

You will find that table topics not only help you refine your speaking skills, they are a lot of fun. The questions in this book can stimulate your imagination and sense of humor. Try some of them at a party. See how they encourage participation and break the ice.

How to Run Table Topics

To run a table topic session, you need the following:
- A topicmaster
- Table topic questions
- A timekeeper
- Timing equipment, including a stopwatch and green, yellow, and red index cards or lights
- A vote counter
- Voting ballots and awards

Topicmaster

Designate one of the people in your group as the topicmaster. The topicmaster does the following:
- Selects the table topic questions to ask.
- Asks for volunteers to come up and answer a question (or "volunteers" people if they are not willing to come up).
- Asks the participant the question.
- Thanks each participant for answering.
- Asks the audience to vote for table topic winners.
- If you have designated a specific portion of a meeting for table topics (like a typical Toastmasters meeting), wraps up the table topics portion and returns control of the meeting to the toastmaster.

Table Topic Questions

The topicmaster can use the questions in this book or create one of his or her own.

The questions are organized into themes. The topicmaster can pick a theme that is appropriate for the time of year like Valentine's

Day questions for a February meeting, or a major event at work like an upcoming conference. Using a theme helps your speakers anticipate the type of questions they will answer, and it helps you prepare or present your questions.

Although we want speakers to have a general idea of what they are going to speak about, we do not want to give them the opportunity to plan their speech in advance. Therefore, we give each speaker a different question and ask the speaker to pick a question at random. Some ways to have a speaker to pick a question include:

- Have the speaker pick a number. (All of the table topic questions in this book are numbered.)
- Put each question on a slip of paper, and have the speaker pick one out of a hat.

The questions in this book are in groups of 12–20, enough to provide you with 15–40 minutes of table topics. You do not have to go through all the questions in each group if you do not have the time. You can save any unasked questions for later.

Timekeeper and Timing Equipment

Designate another member of your group to be the timekeeper. The timekeeper times the speeches, indicates how much time the speaker has spoken, and notes when a speaker has gone overtime.

To keep and indicate the time, you need the following equipment:

- A stopwatch (or a watch or smartphone with a stopwatch feature)
- Green, yellow, and red time indicators, which are either colored index cards or lights.

You can purchase automatic timing lights from Toastmasters International and other sources. Apps are also available for smartphones and tablets. (See "Timing Apps" on page 93 for a list.)

The timekeeper displays the time indicators at the following times. The indicator remains up or on until the timekeeper switches to the next one.

Time (in minutes:seconds)	Indicator to display
1:00	Green
1:30	Yellow
2:00	Red

This is the same timing used for Toastmasters table topics contests.

At 2:30, the speaker has gone over time. You have several options about what to do when the speaker has gone over (besides giving them the hook):

- For beginning speakers, turn off the light or put down the indicator, but allow the speaker to continue. This provides the speaker with a gentle reminder that they have gone over.
- For more experienced speakers, ring a bell or start applause (similar to what televised awards shows do to long acceptance speakers). This provides a firmer reminder that the speaker has gone over.
- For speech contests, timekeepers give no indication that a speaker has gone over, but notes that the speaker is disqualified.

Table topics teach speakers how to be brief, so it is important for speakers to know how much time they have used. As speakers become familiar with the timing, they will learn to structure their speeches to fit.

Vote Counter, Voting Ballots, and Awards

To provide the speakers with feedback and encourage healthy competition, have the audience vote for table topic awards. Designate one person as a vote counter.

You can present one or more awards. Here are some ideas:

- Best table topics
- Most persuasive
- Most improved
- Best humor
- Best gestures
- Best organization

The award can be a ribbon or certificate that the winner can keep, or a perpetual trophy that the winner can display at his or her office or home and bring back at the next meeting. You can purchase ribbons, certificates, and trophies from the Toastmasters catalog.

How to Answer Table Topic Questions

Now, let's look at the other side of a table topic session – how to answer those questions.

To answer a table topic question, follow these steps:
1. Make sure that you understand the question.
2. Select what you are going to cover.
3. Organize your thoughts.
4. Deliver your speech.

Step 1: Understand the Question

Make sure you understand the question before answering it. This sounds logical, but think of the times you asked someone a question and received a wrong answer because the speaker made an incorrect assumption about what you want. Here are some tips to help you understand the question.

Listen Carefully

Listen carefully to all of the words in the question, especially the negatives. Consider these two questions:

- Are there some limitations that a person can change?
- Are there some limitations that a person can never change?

These questions call for different answers. If you are not paying attention and skip "never," you will wind up giving the wrong answer.

Wait

Wait until the person has finished asking the question before formulating an answer. You have seen game shows where a contestant shouts out an answer before the host finished asking the question, and that contestant turns out to be wrong because the clue is in the part the host had not yet asked.

Listen to all parts of the question. Consider the difference between the following:

- Where would you like to go on a trip?
- Where would you like to go on a trip if you had unlimited time and money?
- Where would you like to go on a trip if you could only go on a weekend?

All of these questions require different responses. If you stopped listening after "Where would you like to go on a trip" and did not hear the rest of the question, you might wind up giving a wrong response.

Listen to Background Information

Listen to the background information when it is included in a question. We may ignore this information because we consider it irrelevant. Information that might not seem relevant to you is important to the person asking. By including it in your response, you show consideration to the person asking you – which benefits you if you are trying to persuade the questioner.

Suppose the topicmaster is a military history buff and asks you the following question:

> In the Battle of Gettysburg, General Meade of the Union Army had the opportunity to destroy the army of General Lee when it was blocked from escaping back to Virginia. Instead of attacking Lee, Meade enabled Lee's army to escape. What do you feel should be done when someone like this fails to perform to expectations?

Could you answer the question without the background information? Yes. But think of how much stronger your response will be for the person asking you if you include information about the Battle of Gettysburg in your response. If you do not know what happened, you can describe it in your own words, "I am not as well versed in military history as you, but I know what I would do if I were President Lincoln and faced that situation..." Any way you incorporate background information into your response, you show respect to the topicmaster and earn the appreciation of your audience.

Ask Again and for Clarification

Make sure that you understand the question before answering. If you are unclear about the question, ask that person to repeat the question or rephrase any part of the question you do not understand.

For example, misunderstandings can come from cultural differences. If someone asks, "What is your favorite football team and why?" the answer could be the Tampa Bay Buccaneers (if you are talking about American football) or Manchester United (if you are talking about the football everyone else in the world plays. In that case, you would be talking about your favourite team.) Or, if you do not follow sports at all, you might give that person a blank stare. Ask for an explanation if you are confused or uncertain.

Step 2: Select What You Are Going to Cover

When you choose what you are going to cover in any speech, regardless of time, you have two options:

- Breadth: Cover many subjects briefly.
- Depth: Cover a few subjects in detail.

Suppose you are asked, "What do you enjoy eating?" You can answer in the following ways:

Breadth	I enjoy lots of different foods, but mostly, I'm a carbohydrate lover. My favorites include pasta, rice, and breads of all kinds, including pita, whole wheat…
Depth	I love fudge. Not just any fudge, but the fudge my mother used to make for Christmas. Every November, right after Thanksgiving, my mother would start buying the ingredients…

Which approach should you use for table topics? It depends on the type of question. If you have a long list of items to mention in your response, go with breadth. In a table topics speech, you have time to cover two or three subjects briefly. If you have lots of interesting stories or details you want to share, pick a subject and cover it in depth. One to two minutes isn't a lot of time, so be selective in how much information to cover. With practice, you will learn the right amount of breadth and depth you can cover in that short period.

Step 3: Organize Your Thoughts

Organization benefits you and your listeners. It benefits you because it makes the speech easier to organize and to deliver, and it makes your presentation more effective. It benefits your listeners because it helps them follow your talk and find your main point.

Importance of Organization

Think about the last time you heard a disorganized speaker whose ideas seemed to jump all over the place. When you finished listening to that person, do you feel like you understood what was said? Did you come away with any clear ideas? Probably not.

Now, look at this situation from the speaker's perspective. If you were that speaker, would you feel that you've covered everything you needed? Do you feel like you left something out? Do you feel like you've gotten your ideas across to the listener?

When you organize your speech, you make the presentation clear in your own mind so that you can make it clear in your listener's mind. You select which ideas you want to cover and organize them so that the points follow logically. This saves you from worrying whether you have covered everything or if you will lose your place.

Organizing your speech also helps retain your ideas in the minds of your listeners. By presenting your ideas logically, the listener will be able to follow along and understand you. They will get the main point of your talk, and they will be able to take action on your recommendations.

So, before you speak, take those few seconds to organize your thoughts. They will be the most important seconds that you will invest.

General Rule for Organization

The general rule for organizing a speech is:

- Say what you are going to say.
- Say it.
- Say what you just said.

This structure makes it easy to do the following:

- To write your speech. Just pick the points you want to cover, and your speech is half done! Just introduce the idea at the beginning and recap the points at the end.

- To keep track of what you are covering. When you use this structure, you do not need to worry about losing your place or missing a key idea. By introducing your subject in the beginning, you can remember what you plan to cover in the rest of the speech.

- To retain the speech in your listener's minds. We remember through repetition. That is right: We remember through repetition. Repeating adds emphasis and importance, which further reinforces the ideas with your listeners.

Applying Organization to Table Topics

This structure corresponds to the parts of your table topics speech:

Organization Part	Section of the Speech	What to Do
Say what you are going to say	Opening	♦ Repeat the question you were asked. ♦ Answer the question.
Say it	Body	♦ Explain your answer with supporting points.
Say what you just said	Conclusion	♦ Summarize the points you covered. ♦ End with the main idea that you want listeners to take with them

Opening

In the opening, you want to accomplish the following:

- Show that you understand the question. This is why you repeat the question or incorporate it into the answer.
- Answer the question promptly. People do not want to wait for a reply. Delaying your answer does not add dramatic effect; it frustrates your listeners. They will spend the rest of your speech wondering what your answer will be, and they won't fully hear your points. When you give your answer at the beginning, the rest of your speech will make sense to your audience.

In a typical speech, you also list the points you plan to cover. Because table topics speeches are short, you can omit this step.

Body

In the body, you deliver the points that support the answer you gave. For each point, you provide one or more supporting details. These can be examples, stories that illustrate your point of view, background information – anything that illustrates your main points. The details should also describe why the points you discuss led you to the answer you gave.

How much detail should you give? It depends on whether you are covering points in depth or breadth. If you are covering a few points in depth, you might give one or two specific details. If you are covering a lot of points in breadth, you might just list the points without providing any detail.

Conclusion

In the conclusion, you want to accomplish the following:

- Restate or summarize the points you have covered.
- End with the main idea that you want the audience to take with them. It can be a restatement of your answer. If you are giving a persuasive speech, this needs to be your call to action – what you want the audience to do as a result of the information you gave them.

How to Organize Your Speech Quickly

Organization might seem like a lot of work to do in a few seconds, but as you gain experience with table topics, you can have your organization done and start speaking the moment the topicmaster has finished the question. Just follow these steps:

1. Make sure that you understand the question.
2. Think of your answer.
3. Think of the main idea that you want to leave with your audience.
4. Think of the main points to support your answer.
5. If you have only one or two points, think of details to support the points. If you have three or more, skip this step.
6. Put together your organization:
    - Your opening is a restatement of the question followed by your answer.
    - Your body is your supporting points with any details.
    - Your conclusion is your restated answer and a call to action, if desired.
7. Start speaking.

Step 4: Deliver Your Speech

By understanding the question and putting together a well-developed response, you are well on your way to giving a great impromptu speech. As you gain experience, you can add other elements of speaking to make your speech more effective:

- Eye contact (which will be easier because you do not have any notes)
- Vocal variety (including changes in pace and pauses)
- Body language (including gestures and facial expressions)

All of these will come with practice and experience. Here are a few tips to get you started.

Eye Contact

Eye contact is a powerful communications tool. It enables you to connect with your audience, project sincerity and openness, and keep your listener's attention. However, maintaining eye contact can be difficult for some people, and there are some cultural issues to consider when using it. You also want to make sure you use eye contact correctly to project the right non-verbal message.

Consider how long you look into someone's eyes when you speak. For a professional speech, only look directly into someone's eyes for about a second. A longer glance might make someone uncomfortable or could be construed as inappropriate flirting.

If you find yourself nervous about looking people directly in the eye, start small. Just give someone a brief glance or look around their eyes instead of directly into their pupils. With practice, you will become more comfortable with giving people direct eye contact, and you will find your discomfort start to fade.

Consider cultural differences when using eye contact with your listeners. Some cultures appreciate direct eye contact. Others consider it rude. Be aware of the people in your audience and when people seem uncomfortable or start looking away when you look at them.

Vocal Variety

It may seem that a one-to-two minute speech won't give you enough time to add vocal variety. There are ways to add variety in your speech to keep an audience's attention.

The most effective tool for adding variety is the pause. Pauses give the audience a chance to think about what you said. Therefore, a good place to pause is right after you make a key point. Pauses also slow down your pace so that the audience can understand you more. Nervous speakers tend to speak quickly in order to get the speech out of the way. Pausing gives you a chance to breathe, to calm down, and speak at a more controlled pace.

Pauses help eliminate "ahs" and "ums". People use such distracting fillers to give them time to think. Use pauses instead, and your speech will sound more polished and professional.

Subtle changes in volume, tone, and pace can also keep an audience's attention and help you emphasize key points. As you gain more experience, you can find ways to add variety and pauses to your speech.

Body Language

Most communication is non-verbal, so pay attention to how you appear to your audience.

Use good posture, which projects confidence and helps your breathing by opening your chest. Make sure your gestures are relaxed and natural. Avoid distracting motions such as putting your hands in your pockets or playing with your rings. Also avoid repetitive motions that can distract listeners.

To see how your gestures and postures might come across to an audience, try videotaping yourself as you practice. You can identify posture and gesture problems to fix.

Your clothing also sends a message to your listeners. Make sure your clothes are clean and in good repair. Avoid large and flashy jewelry, ties, and scarves that can distract your listeners. As for what to wear, it depends on the situation and your audience. For interviews and formal presentations, wear a good-fitting business suit and comfortable and polished dress shoes. For more informal situations, dress well enough to show authority, but not too fancily that it puts off your listeners. Avoid shorts, tank tops, and other revealing clothing. You want your outfit to project an image your audience will respect.

Additional Tips

For tips on improving your delivery, see your Toastmasters manuals or visit this website:

http://www.matthewarnoldstern.com/speeches/speakingtips.html

Examples

Let us look at some sample responses to table topic questions. Each one is broken down according to the three parts of a table topics response: The answer, the supporting points and details, and a conclusion with a summary and the main idea.

Question: If you can live in any time of history, what would it be and why?

Opening: Answer	If I can live in any time of history, it would be now.
Body: Supporting points and details	We have all heard the curse, "May you live in interesting times." We know that "interesting" is an understatement. War, terrorism, economic troubles, threats of ecological disaster – we face a multitude of crises that certainly make these times interesting.
	But I consider "interesting times" like these a

blessing instead of a curse. While we face a myriad of threats, we are also granted the opportunity to address these dangers, stretch our capabilities, and become better as people as we strive to make the world better.

Every generation has faced grave dangers, and every generation has risen to the challenge to solve them.

In the 1930s and 1940s, we faced a crushing Depression and genocidal dictators. We battled against tyranny and won, and then we ushered in a period of great prosperity and technical innovation.

After World War II, we faced a Cold War and the danger of nuclear annihilation. That generation stepped from the abyss of mutual destruction, made arms control agreements, and learned to channel the competition between superpowers into peaceful activities such as the exploration of space.

Today, we face the specter of global terrorism, dangerous new diseases such as SARS, and ecological destruction. But we also have at our disposal incredible breakthroughs in technology and communications, greater knowledge of genetics, and more appreciation of our global community. We have the power to solve these crises and improve ourselves and our planet, as generations have before us.

Conclusion: Summary and main idea

With all the opportunities that we have available to us, I see our "interesting times" as a blessing, not a curse. I wouldn't want to live in any other time of history except now.

Notice a few things about this table topics speech:

- ◆ At the beginning of the speech, the speaker restated the question and answered it promptly.
- ◆ The speaker built the speech around a well-known saying, "May you live in interesting times" and added a twist by showing why it is a blessing instead of a curse.
- ◆ The supporting points followed a logical progression, describing the Depression and World War II of the 1930s

and 1940s, the Cold War of the 1950s and 1960s, and then brought the topic back to today.

- ♦ The conclusion ties up the speech by referring back to the "interesting times" quote and repeating the answer.

And the speaker did this all in a minute, 55 seconds! See how much information you can pack into a short period of time.

Let us try another one.

Question: If you can pursue one goal and be guaranteed that you cannot fail, what goal would you choose and why?

Opening: Answer	If I could pursue one goal and be guaranteed that I cannot fail, it would be my life-long dream of becoming a successful novelist.
Body: Supporting points and details	For me, being a successful novelist would be more than just publishing a book. There are lots of writers who get published, only to see their years of work get tossed into the remainder bin.
	For me, becoming a successful novelist means producing books that sell – and sell millions, because that is what publishers demand. And not just one book, but a whole series of books. Book, after book, after book. I want to see people lining up at the bookstores at midnight waiting for my next work, just like they do for J.K. Rowling.
	And there is something else I want just like J.K. Rowling – merchandising. We went to the optician the other day. Do you know what type of eyeglasses they had there? Harry Potter glasses. That's right, J.K. Rowling gets paid every time some kid sticks Harry Potter on his or her face.
	So, did someone offer J.K. Rowling the same deal, the promise that if she could pursue her goal of becoming the creator of Harry Potter and his friends and foes at Hogwarts that she would not fail? I think so. More precisely, she made up her mind that she would pursue her goal and would not fail.
	Remember, when she started writing Harry Potter, she was a struggling single mother, writing her first drafts on whatever scrap paper she could find. How ludicrous it would be to believe back then that she would become wealthier than Queen Elizabeth and the most powerful author in publishing. Yet, she

	made up her mind that she would not fail, and guaranteed that success through hard work and perseverance.
Conclusion: Summary and main idea	The notion that someone could pursue a goal and be guaranteed not to fail is no fantasy. I believe it is possible, as J.K. Rowling has shown. And I believe that I can fulfill my dream of becoming a successful novelist.

Notice a few things about this table topics speech:

- Again, the speaker restated the question and answered it promptly.
- The speaker clarified the answer by providing details about what that person defines as a "successful novelist."
- The speaker used J.K. Rowling as a pivot, moving from a description of a successful novelist to what it takes to become successful. Here, the speaker not only answers the question but validates the answer by showing how it is possible to set a goal and achieve it.
- The conclusion includes the speaker's main points: it is possible to pursue dreams and be assured success, and that the speaker can become a successful novelist.

A very powerful and convincing argument – in a mere minute and 47 seconds.

Now, you are ready to start asking and answering your own table topics questions.

Workplace Questions

Most Toastmasters are working adults. The following questions relate to workplace situations that most Toastmasters can relate to. These questions work especially well in lunchtime and company clubs.

If I Were in Charge

Ask your participants about their philosophy about leadership.

1. What do you think is the most important quality that a leader should have?
2. Give us an example of someone you think is an exceptional leader.
3. Tell us about your first experience in being a leader.
4. What do you think is the most difficult problem a leader faces?
5. How do you motivate uninspired and uncooperative people?
6. Which leadership skill do you feel you need to work on the most?
7. Delegation is one of the most important things a leader needs to do. What do you think is the most important key to successful delegation?
8. How has being in Toastmasters helped your leadership skills?
9. You've heard the old saying, "Rank has its privileges." Do you agree with this or not and why?
10. Good leaders are often good mentors. Tell us about a mentor who influenced you the most.
11. Suppose you are in charge of a project. One of the members of your team fails to do his or her task on time and causes the project to miss its schedule. How would you handle the situation?
12. What can be done to get more women into leadership roles and government and industry?
13. You've heard the saying, "Power corrupts." What do you think can be done to prevent power from corrupting someone?
14. According to the Dilbert Principle, the most incompetent employees of a company go to where they can do the least harm – management. Do you agree with that statement? Why or why not?

Interview Questions

Nothing tests your impromptu speaking skills more than a job interview. Job interviews don't only happen when you apply for a new job. You may be interviewed when you're considered for a promotion or to take on a new assignment. You may also find yourself being interviewed when a company plans to reorganize or considers who to keep in a planned reduction in force. Always be ready for interviews with questions like these.

1. "Why do you feel you're qualified for this position?"
2. "Where do you see yourself in the next five years?"
3. "What was your greatest accomplishment at your last job?"
4. "What do you feel is your greatest weakness and how do you work with it?"
5. "How do you learn new skills?"
6. "From your perspective, how does your job fit with the overall goals of our organization?"
7. "Tell us about something you did that helped a company's bottom line."
8. "How do you typically handle conflicts with other employees?"
9. "What is your experience with working with people in different countries and different cultures?"
10. "Who do you feel is the most important person in the company and why?"
11. "How do you deal with angry customers?"
12. "If I hire you, what would you do in the first 30 days of your employment here?"
13. "What is your idea of the perfect workplace?"
14. "What would cause you to leave an employer?"
15. "What is it about this job and this company that made you want to apply here?"

Spin Doctors

A number of people have the unpleasant responsibility of putting a positive spin on bad news. Such people are known as spin doctors. With these questions, you can stretch your imagination and have fun in trying to present negative news in a positive light.

1. You are a representative of the Hell Tourism Commission. Tell us why Hell should be our number one vacation destination.
2. It's April, 1912, and you are a public relations representative for the White Star Lines. It turns out that one of your ships, the HMS *Titanic*, had a slight altercation with an iceberg and went down to the bottom of the Atlantic along with 1,500 of your paying customers. You are facing a group of anxious and demanding reporters who insist on hearing your side of the story.
3. You are the agent of a star baseball player. He has been found to be in violation of the league's restrictions against performance-enhancing drugs and has been suspended for 80 games. Explain your client's situation to the press.
4. You are Lord Cornwallis. You just arrived home in England after surrendering to the Americans at Yorktown. King George III has called you into his chamber demanding why the most powerful, highly trained, and well-equipped army in Europe couldn't beat that motley group of tax-hating colonial rabble-rousers.
5. You are a precocious six-year-old. You just broke your mother's favorite lamp. Explain yourself to her.
6. You are the producer of the new movie, *Let's Blow Up Lots of Stuff*. However, the movie blew up in the box office: It only earned $15,000 its opening weekend, and the movie cost $100 million to make. You are being interviewed by an entertainment industry trade magazine. Explain your situation.
7. You are a customer service representative for an airline. Your furious customers want to know why they arrived at Orange County, California and their luggage arrived in Port Au Prince, Haiti.
8. You are a district attorney who just lost a high-profile murder case. You had plenty of evidence to prosecute, but the accused got off on a legal technicality. You are addressing reporters at the steps of the courthouse just after the verdict.
9. You are the coach of your local sports team, and your team was just beaten badly by your opponents. You are being interviewed by your local sports reporter after the game.

10. You are Jack. You have just traded your family's only cow for a bag of magic beans. Explain yourself to your wife.
11. You have been hired by the Cow Brain Advisory Board to put together an ad campaign to convince people to start adding cow brains to their meals. How would you encourage the public that cow brains are a wonderful delicacy?
12. You are the campaign manager of a flamboyant and outspoken congressional candidate. At a talk show, your candidate made some candid and disparaging remarks about your opponent and a certain ethnic group. How do you respond?
13. It's November, 1948. You are the editor of the *Chicago Tribune* that published the "Dewey Defeats Truman" headline when it was Truman who got reelected. Explain yourself to your publisher.
14. You are seven years old. Your mom gave you $5.00 to buy milk, bread, and butter. Instead, you bought gum, baseball cards, and ice cream. Explain yourself to your mom.

Status Report

A key business skill is the ability to give information succinctly and accurately. These questions will help participants practice. So that participants don't disclose confidential company information, they should use their imagination and make up responses.

1. "I know the project you're working on is complex. Skip the details and just give me a brief summary."
2. "What would prevent our product from shipping on time?"
3. "Sales have been slow, and we might not be able to make our quota this quarter. What do you think we can do to close more deals?"
4. "Can you explain why that information is missing from the user's manual?"
5. "We've been having problems getting answers from our office in London. How can we get them to be more responsive?"
6. "What do you need in order to complete your section of the report?"
7. "I'm the new CEO. Tell me about your job and how you contribute to the company."
8. "Why do you feel you deserve a raise?"
9. "So, you finished interviewing the candidates for the job opening. Who should we make an offer to and why?"
10. "This design flaw has cost our company a lot of business and caused a lot of negative publicity. Why wasn't this problem caught before we shipped?"
11. "What features do our competitors have in their product that ours lack?"
12. "What are you planning to do today?"
13. "What are your goals for this week, and what is your progress on them?"
14. "I'm concerned that the task won't be done correctly. How are you making sure that it's done right?"
15. "Why do you think it is a bad idea for us to pursue this option?"

Convince Me

Another key business skill is to convince others to adopt your point of view. In this exercise, participants imagine that they are in a business meeting where they have to convince others to agree with their ideas. So that participants don't disclose confidential company information, they should use their imagination and make up responses.

1. The software you want the company to purchase will improve productivity. However, your boss wants to purchase less expensive software, even though it is not as easy to use, and it has known bugs. Convince your manager to consider the product you recommend.
2. You and another candidate are being considered for a promotion. Tell your manager why she should choose you.
3. Your company hired an outside ad agency to come up with a campaign for a new product. You feel the ads don't get the message across, and you worry that some images might be considered offensive. However, some executives are enthralled by its imagery and others worry about wasting the money they've already spent by not using their campaign. Convince the executive board to change their minds.
4. Convince your company to start a Toastmasters club.
5. Sales in Latin America have been consistently below projections. As director of regional sales, you believe that if you could go to the sales office in Santiago, Chile, you can find out what the problem is and fix it. Your vice president doesn't want to spend the money for a trip and some executives want to lay off the entire team and start fresh. Convince the executives to send you on this trip.
6. As CEO, you signed the agreement for your company to be purchased by a larger firm. Now, you have to reassure your employees and convince them that this merger is for the best.
7. The coffee that used to be served in your break room has been replaced with a less expensive brand. Reassure your employees that this is a good thing.
8. Your CEO publicly announced his stand on a controversial issue. As a department manager, you know that some of your employees strongly oppose his position. You have to keep your employees calm and focused on their work.
9. Your IT department has to choose between different brands of smartphones. Convince them to select with the brand you prefer.
10. Your CEO has been caught in a personal scandal that has caused public outrage and affected your company's sales and stock price.

    The board of directors has asked you, as senior vice president, to convince the CEO to resign.
11. The product you have been developing still has major bugs to fix, but the executives want to ship it anyway. Convince them not to ship it right now.
12. The company wants to get rid of an old product that still has a strong and loyal customer base. Convince the executive board that the product should continue to be offered and can be retooled to make more money.
13. You evaluated three different sites for a new office. The first has the lowest rent, but it would mean a longer and less convenient commute for most of your employees. The second is in a convenient location and has low rent, but it would require extensive renovations before you can move in. The third is a beautiful office in a prestigious location, which your CEO prefers, but it has the highest rent and least amount of office space. Pick a site and make your recommendations to the board.
14. Your team just completed a difficult project, and you want to reward them by giving them a day off. Ask your director for approval.

Bad Ideas

History is full of bad ideas that in retrospect we can say, "What the heck were they thinking!?" The reason why so many bad ideas get implemented is because someone has convinced the decision makers that the bad idea was a great idea. The challenge for your participants is to convince people that your bad idea is a good one that they should follow through on.

1. It's 1954, and you're presenting your idea for a new car to the Board of Directors of the Ford Motor Company. The car is called the Edsel. Tell the Board of Directors why you think Ford should build this car.
2. You are in the third grade. Convince one of your classmates to play hooky from school.
3. You are a marketing manager for a software manufacturer. Convince the members of your project to ship the latest version of your software, even though it has well-known and potentially serious bugs.
4. You are a real estate agent. The property you are showing your clients needs a new roof, new carpet, new interior and exterior paint, has significant termite damage, master bathroom plumbing that doesn't work, and is located near a toxic-waste dump. Convince your clients to buy it.
5. You are the CEO of a company that is trying to get an initial stock offering off the ground. You learn of a way to "cook the books" to make the company look like it's earning more than it actually is and therefore boost the stock price. Convince the other corporate officers that the company can get away with it, and therefore, should do it.
6. You are Napoleon. Tell your generals why they should continue their campaign in Russia even though it is the dead of winter.
7. You are an executive for a food manufacturer. Tell us why the public will go gaga for your new flavor of ice cream, mackerel.
8. You meet an old friend from high school. He seems miserable because his business is failing, he's heavily in debt, and is on the verge of bankruptcy. On the other hand, you are rolling in cash, have a new luxury electric vehicle, and a $125,000 diamond watch. This is all from your line of work: drug dealing. Convince your friend that you can help him out of his money problems by joining you in this line of work.
9. It's 1973, and you are a movie studio executive. A young filmmaker named George Lucas pitched an idea to you for a movie called *Star Wars*. Tell us why you turned him down.

10. You are an entrepreneur with a hot idea for a new franchise business: Surgery to Go. Patients would drive in, have surgery done in their car, and drive off. You even have a slogan, "Quadruple bypass in one hour, or it's free!!" Tell a group of investors why they should put money into your business.
11. You know your customers can't afford that brand new sports car you're selling them at your dealership. Convince them to buy it anyway.
12. You are 16. Convince your older brother or sister to buy you and your friends some beer.

Recovery

An important business skill is learning how to recover after a failure. As participants share their stories, they can teach and inspire others to recover from their setbacks.

1. What was the biggest mistake you ever made in the workplace?
2. Share with us your biggest comeback story.
3. Are there mistakes that are so grievous that a person can never recover?
4. Most successful business leaders have had major failures. Tell us about such a leader who inspires you.
5. Would you hire someone who had been convicted of a felony, even if it were for a non-violent crime and the person has been paroled?
6. You apologized to someone you offended, but that person doesn't accept your apology. What do you do?
7. How would you comfort someone who feels remorseful about a mistake he or she made?
8. A member of your staff made a major mistake that cost your company money and put you on the hot seat with upper management. What do you do?
9. A company is about to hire you, but a background check found inappropriate pictures of you that were posted on social media years ago. What do you do?
10. Have you ever been terminated or laid off from a job? What did you do?
11. What do you do when you feel discouraged by a work situation?
12. How do you earn back someone's trust after you let him or her down?

Dealing with Hostility

Angry customers, difficult coworkers, and nasty trolls on social media. We all have to deal with hostility at our workplaces. These questions challenge you to think about how you would deal with difficult – and sometimes dangerous – situations.

1. You're a supervisor at a retail store. You see a customer screaming vulgarities at your clerk at the register. Other customers are staring at the person. One potential customer rushed out the door with her children. How do you deal with the situation?
2. You moderate the company's social media page. Someone keeps posting nasty messages about your company and other customers on your page. You delete the messages and block the poster, but that person creates new accounts and posts more hateful messages on your page and other sites. What do you do next?
3. One of your company's executives deals with others in a bullying manner. He raises his voice, steps up close to employees and stares them down, and threatens employees with termination if they don't give into him. You have to work with this executive on a new project. What do you do?
4. A customer asks you to do something that violates company rules. When you politely decline, the customer gets furious at you. How do you respond?
5. While passing through the hallway, you overhear an employee saying, "If she chews me out one more time, I swear I'm going to kill her!" What do you do?
6. You lose your temper in a meeting. How do you recover from the situation?
7. A customer at your store seems to be acting erratically. He wanders around the store mumbling angrily to himself. He keeps his hands in his pockets. You think he's holding something in there, but you're not sure. What do you do?
8. An employee in the cubicle across from you is always on the phone, and he always talks loudly and profanely to the point that it distracts you from your work. What do you do?
9. You're a teacher. Two of your students start fighting in your classroom. What do you do?
10. On social media, you come across the page for one of your coworkers. You're shocked to see how bitterly and frequently your coworker complains about her job. She even posts "I ought to burn that place to the ground!" What do you do?

11. You are treated rudely by an employee of one of your suppliers. How do you respond?
12. You catch a senior director doing something inappropriate. She warns, "If you tell anyone, I'll have you fired!" What do you do?
13. You are working with a colleague from another country. That person treats you in a way you consider rude and inappropriate, but it is consistent with the culture of that country. How do you respond?
14. A coworker makes a racist remark. How do you react?
15. At a company party, one of your coworkers had too much to drink. When another person tries to help him, he gets belligerent and throws a punch at him. You're close by as this happens. What do you do?

Global Business

In today's global workplace, you have to interact with people from around the world. These questions ask participants how they would deal with people from different countries and cultures.

1. How do you arrange a meeting with people in different time zones?
2. Do you think people must learn English to be able to do business globally?
3. Should international travel be required for employees on global teams?
4. How do you work with people who have difficulty communicating in your language?
5. What was your most memorable business trip?
6. When visiting another country, you make a major cultural faux pas. What do you do?
7. What advice would you give to someone who wants to learn another language?
8. Employees from another country are coming to your office. Where do you like to take them out to eat?
9. What is your favorite country to visit for business?
10. Have cultural differences ever made it difficult for you to work with someone else? How did you resolve the problem?
11. Do you think employees should be allowed to bring their families with them when they travel abroad?
12. Would you ever refuse to do business with people in another country because of things that nation did in the past?
13. What foreign food or drink do you wish they sold in your country?
14. What advice would you give to business travelers coming to your country?
15. How do you deal with jet lag?

Executive Decision

Scenarios of situations leaders might need to face in today's business environment.

1. You are hiring a new employee, and you have to choose between two candidates. One is a recognized leader in the field, an exceptional worker, and someone can make a great contribution to the department. But she wants $15,000 a year more than you are budgeted for this position. The other candidate is eager, but inexperienced and would need considerable training to become fully efficient. However, he is within the lower third of your budgeted salary range. Who would you hire and why?
2. A website posted a rumor about a large company buying your firm. When you asked members of the executive committee about the rumor, they would not "confirm or deny" anything. Meanwhile, your employees spend their time gossiping, updating their resumes, and seeming more and more demoralized. What do you do?
3. Alison is the most cheerful, good-natured, and productive member of your department. But lately, she has been sullen, withdrawn, and short-tempered, and the quality of her work is tapering off. One of your female employees saw her crying in the bathroom one day. The office gossip is that Alison is going through a divorce. What do you do?
4. You can add a new technology to your product that has the *potential* of doubling your sales, but it would be incompatible with the systems used by a third of your existing customers. What do you recommend?
5. Your company is downsizing. You have a staff of five, and the executive committee requires that you lay off one of them. How do you decide which person to lay off?
6. You are an engineering manager. You've been very flexible about what time employees come in and come out, as long as they get the work done. In particular, you have a brilliant engineer who comes in at "the crack of noon," but will work into the wee hours of the morning. However, you now have a new director who insists that employees work "core hours" starting at 9:00 A.M. and threatens to discipline employees who arrive to work late. What do you do?
7. Pete is your top salesperson. In a recent random company drug test, he turned out positive for cocaine. What do you do?

8. With a few weeks before your scheduled release date, Dave, the marketing whiz, tells you to add a new feature to the product. He says that without the new feature, the product will be quickly outdated and sales will fall short. Adding the feature would add another month to the schedule. How do you respond?

9. You are the engineering director in a meeting with the heads of other departments. Suddenly, the vice president of support starts berating you about the quality of the company's products. In his outburst, he not only questions your department's quality, but yours and your employees' intelligence and parentage. How do you respond?

10. You receive an e-mail from one of your employees that has critical information about your chief competitor – information that can affect a product you are currently developing. You ask the employee where he got the information. He beams and says proudly that he has cracked into the competitor's network and can obtain their confidential company information at will. What will you do with the employee and with the information you received?

11. Alex desperately wants to transfer into your department. He likes what your department does, and he is qualified to do the work. However, the main reason he wants to transfer is because he is unhappy with his current boss. He says she is a picky micromanager who keeps him from getting his work done. Later, Alex's boss calls you about his proposed transfer. She tells you not to accept him because he won't follow directions, and he has a bad attitude. Would you let Alex transfer into your department?

12. You have been recently promoted to manager of a department suffering from severe internal conflicts. The department is divided into two cliques. The previous manager favored one clique over the other, which increased the hostility among the employees. Because of the internal turmoil, other groups have refused to work with this department and have developed procedural workarounds so they don't have to. Overall, the department feels devalued, divided, distrustful, and demoralized. What do you to rebuild this group?

Breaking the News

We often have to give difficult news. For each of these exercises, role play what you would say to someone in the following situations.

1. You have to tell a customer that you won't be able to fix his computer for two more weeks because a part you need has been backordered.
2. The deadline for your development team has been moved in by a week. The product must be ready to demonstrate to a prospective customer on Friday. You must tell the team.
3. Your employee has shown consistently poor work performance and has been absent frequently. You need to give the employee a written disciplinary warning.
4. The piece of software that your offshore development team in Serbia has produced does not match your specifications. It needs considerable rework. You need to conduct a teleconference with them.
5. The company you are contracting for demands significant changes to your project that they never brought up in any meeting. They are threatening not to pay you unless you make those changes by the deadline, which is coming up in three days. They are waiting for your response.
6. You are resigning from the company because you accepted an offer from a competing firm. What do you tell your boss?
7. You are the company president. Your company has suffered major losses, and you need to have a seven percent layoff of your staff. You are about to speak at your company meeting.
8. The founder of your company has just died. Even worse: He died in a hotel room, and the woman he was with is not his wife. You are giving the news at a company meeting.
9. You have learned that one of your company's products has a serious mechanical defect that can cause injury or death. The defect can be easily and permanently fixed, but it would require a public recall of 25,000 units to correct the problem. You are in your company president's office to give the news and your recommendation.
10. Your boss' micromanagement, verbal browbeating of staff, and frequently off-color language is hurting your team's morale and productivity. Your team has begged you to speak to him.
11. Your company landed a major government contract that will double your revenue. This means money for bonuses but

overtime to deliver product on time. Make the news to your employees.

12. You are the gate attendant for an airline. The flight out of Denver has been delayed until tomorrow morning because of bad weather. What do you say to the passengers?

13. A laptop has been stolen from one of your conference rooms. Evidence is pointing to someone within the company. How do you tell your staff?

14. Senior management wants all managers to crack down on "unauthorized Web surfing" during work hours. You haven't had a problem with your staff using the Internet, and you do a little browsing on eBay yourself. What do you say to your staff?

Career Choices

I wrote these questions originally for a meeting of the Society for Technical Communication (STC), but I adapted them to fit most professions.

1. What advice would you give someone who wants to pursue your type of career?
2. What was the greatest disappointment in your career and what did you learn from it?
3. Every job contributes something to society. What contribution do you think your job offers?
4. What do you think is the most important skill that every person in your profession should have should have and why?
5. Do you feel that people in your line of work receive the pay and respect that they deserve? Why or why not?
6. How do you think your profession will change in the next ten years?
7. Technology has changed the work in all professions. How has it changed yours?
8. It seems like every office has some sort of goody table with treats on it. What is your favorite snack at the office?
9. If you had the budget to go to any conference or offsite training course you want, which one would you go to and why?
10. Most employees are concerned about their job security in today's economy. What advice would you give to people in your profession who want to hold onto their jobs?
11. What was the proudest moment of your career?
12. What book do you think should be on the desk of every person who works in your career?

Special Seasons and Events Questions

New Years. Birthdays. Christmas. We all have holidays and special events that roll along the calendar. This section has table topic questions appropriate for meetings before these special events.

The questions listed here are for United States holidays, but you can adapt them to fit the holidays and special occasions in your country.

Happy New Year!

Start the New Year with these questions.

1. Do you think January really is the perfect month to start a new year?
2. What will you miss about last year?
3. Give us a prediction for the new year.
4. What is your main new year's resolution?
5. What was the best New Year's Eve you ever celebrated?
6. Tell us one way you have changed in the previous year.
7. Losing weight is a popular new year's resolution, but why is it so hard for most people to lose weight?
8. The Tournament of Roses Parade in Pasadena, California is a great New Year's Day tradition. If you could create a float for the parade, what would it be?
9. If you can go anywhere to celebrate New Year's Eve, where would you go and what would you do?
10. How did you celebrate New Year's Day last year?
11. If you can create a new custom for New Year's Day, what would it be?
12. A friend had too much to drink on New Year's Eve and begs you for a hangover remedy. What would you tell your friend?
13. Tell us about an event that you're looking forward to in the coming year.
14. Some families have get-togethers on New Year's Day. Tell us about your favorite family get-together.

Winter Questions

Some questions to warm up cold winter days.

1. What is your favorite cold-weather drink?
2. Most people like to eat soup on cold days. What soup is your favorite?
3. Some areas have "snow days" when the snowfall is so heavy, schools have to close. How would you keep kids busy on those days?
4. Why do you think every snowflake is unique?
5. What is your favorite Winter Olympics sport?
6. What do you typically do when you come down with a cold or flu?
7. What is your favorite cold weather outfit?
8. An alien from another planet asks you, "What is ice and how do you make it?" Answer him.
9. What is the coldest you have ever been?
10. In the movie *Frozen*, a queen has the power to make ice and snow on command. What would you do if you had that power?
11. Would you ever want to live in a place that never has a winter?
12. Many people like to escape the winter by going on vacation to someplace warm. What is your favorite place for a sunny getaway?

Isn't It Romantic?

Questions for Valentine's Day, Sweetheart's Day, or any special romantic event on your calendar.

1. Tell us about the first person you kissed.
2. What is your fondest Valentine's Day memory?
3. Tell us about the best date you ever went on.
4. What does love mean to you?
5. What is the most romantic movie you have ever seen?
6. Tell us what you're going to do for your loved one on Valentine's Day.
7. What advice would you give to someone who has just been dumped by a boyfriend or girlfriend?
8. How old do you think a young man or woman should be before they start dating?
9. Tell us your idea of a romantic getaway.
10. Why are celebrity marriages usually so short?
11. What is your favorite Valentine's candy?
12. Do you believe that love conquers all?
13. What do you think makes for a perfect relationship?
14. Did you go to your high-school prom? Tell us about it.
15. Who was your first love? What was this person like?

Spring

For most people, spring is the time for new beginnings, romance, and enjoying the outdoors. These questions encourage speakers to talk about their feelings about spring.

1. Tell us what you *dislike* about spring.
2. Spring is when the flowers start blooming. What is your favorite flower and why?
3. Why do you think spring is considered a time for romance?
4. Spring is the start of baseball season. What are your thoughts about baseball?
5. Do you plan to do any spring cleaning? If so, what do you plan to clean?
6. In the other half of the world, spring starts six months from now. How would you feel if you have to wait another six months for spring?
7. Warm weather means outdoor fun! What is your favorite outdoor activity?
8. Spring means putting away winter clothes. Which winter outfit will you miss?
9. Easter and Passover as well as other religious and cultural holidays take place in the spring. What is your favorite spring holiday and how do you celebrate it?
10. Anne Bradstreet wrote, "If we had no winter, the spring would not be so pleasant." What does this mean to you?
11. Tell us about your most memorable spring.
12. Spring fever is when we feel lazy or restless as the weather gets nicer. What do you think is the cure for spring fever?

Mother's and Father's Days

Most countries have special days to honor and celebrate parents. Here are some questions about how you celebrate your parents.

1. What was the best gift you ever gave your mother or father?
2. Why do children usually give their mothers better gifts than their fathers?
3. What would you like your kids to do for you on your special day?
4. Which do you prefer on your special day, to have a home-cooked meal or have someone take you out to a restaurant?
5. Tell us about someone who was like a parent to you.
6. What was the best thing your parents ever did for you?
7. Many kids like to give handmade gifts to their parents. What is the best handmade gift you've ever given or received?
8. What was your most memorable Mother's or Father's Day?
9. Come up with a new tradition to celebrate parents.
10. Some say you should always honor your parents. Some say you should only honor your parents when they deserve it. What do you think?
11. What do you look for when you shop for a greeting card for your mother or father?
12. Tell us about a Mother's or Father's Day tradition in your family.

Graduation

You have been asked to be a commencement speaker for the school described in the question. Tell the audience what you are going to say. (Two minutes isn't long enough for a full commencement speech, though most graduates would like you to keep it to that long.)

1. You are the commencement speaker at Harvard Law School. What would you say in your speech?
2. Two weeks ago, one of the most popular students at the high school you have been asked to speak at drowned in a surfing accident. What would you say at the class' graduation?
3. You are addressing the graduating class at Creative Playtime preschool. What wisdom would you impart to these students as they venture forth to kindergarten?
4. You have been asked to speak at the graduation at your city's police academy. What would you say to these new officers?
5. Your country's top medical school has asked you to speak at their commencement. What would you say to those new doctors?
6. You are speaking at the high school where you graduated. What would you say to the members of this year's graduating class?
7. Earlier this year at the high school where you are speaking, a student went on a shooting rampage and killed several students and wounded a dozen more. A number of those wounded students are in the graduating class. What would you say to them and the rest of the class in your speech?
8. You have been chosen to be the commencement speaker at Clown College. What would you say to the new group of circus clowns?
9. Because of budget cuts, the junior high school where you are speaking is closing after this year. You are speaking to the last graduating class this school will have. What will you say?
10. You are the guest speaker at a naturalization ceremony, where a group of immigrants are officially becoming citizens. What would you say to them?
11. Picture yourself back in high school. If you were asked to give the valedictorian speech at your high school graduation, what would you have said?
12. You are speaking at a brand new high school to the school's first graduating class. What would you say?
13. You are addressing an obviously bored and restless elementary school graduating class after it sat through a long and dull speech by the school's principal. What will you do for your speech?

14. You are addressing the graduation of a troubled high school that has been plagued by drugs, gang violence, teenage pregnancy, and racial tension. The graduating class is the 70% who didn't drop out when they started high school, and it's questionable whether many of them have the skills to succeed in life. What type of commencement address would you give to this class?
15. You have gotten an invitation to address the students of the Undertakers Academy as they complete their training to become morticians. What speech would you give to this group?

Summer

Here are perfect warm-weather questions.

1. What is your favorite summertime outfit?
2. Which of the summer blockbuster movies are you planning to see?
3. What is your most favorite memory of a summer vacation you had when you were a child?
4. Will the higher prices in gasoline affect your summer driving plans?
5. How do you keep cool when it is very hot outside?
6. What would be your ideal summer vacation?
7. What is the hottest place (in terms of temperature) that you've ever been?
8. Rolling blackouts occasionally happen in summer. How will you cope if a rolling blackout hits?
9. For many, summer means barbecue. Tell us about the best barbecue you ever attended.
10. The kids will be out of school for the summer. What suggestions can you give for keeping them occupied?
11. What summer TV shows do you like to watch?
12. Do you like going to the beach? Why or why not?
13. Tell us about what you don't like about summer.
14. How are you planning to save on electricity this summer?
15. What was the worst summer vacation you had?

The Post-September 11 World

September 11, 2001 has changed the perspective of everyone in the world. For Americans and people in other Western countries, September 11 shattered a sense of security. For people in countries that have already been scarred by terrorism, September 11 reinforced their understanding about the dangers of terror. These questions are appropriate for the anniversary of this event or for the terrorist attacks that have happened since.

1. Where were you on September 11, 2001? If you were not born yet or were too young to remember, what did your parents do?
2. A memorial, museum, and new office buildings were built on the former World Trade Center site. Do you think this was an appropriate use of the land?
3. How do you think the world has changed since September 11, 2001?
4. People have birthdays and wedding anniversaries on September 11. How should people celebrate those events when that date has such a tragic connection?
5. How would you explain what the world was like before September 11, 2001 to people who were born after it happened?
6. Have you changed or cancelled travel plans because of your concern about terrorism?
7. Do you think the terrorist threat is overrated?
8. Would you read a book or watch a movie about September 11? Why or why not?
9. All professional sports leagues in the United States cancelled their events the weekend immediately after September 11. Was this a good idea?
10. What preparations do you think people should make in anticipation of future terrorist attacks?
11. What response do you think the United States should have made in the aftermath of September 11?
12. How do you think the perception of the events of September 11 has changed in the years since it happened?
13. How do you think future generations should remember September 11?
14. What do you think you can do personally to prevent terrorism?
15. Do you feel safer from terrorism today than you did five years ago?

It's Spooky

Most cultures have a holiday that reminds people of their mortality. In the United States, it is Halloween (which tends to be focused on eating candy and watching scary movies). The following questions fit a Halloween theme or whenever you are in a spooky mood.

1. Do you believe in ghosts? Why or why not?
2. What was the most frightening movie you've ever seen?
3. Which celebrity frightens you the most?
4. Tell us about a phobia you have. If you don't have one, make one up.
5. When you were a kid, what scared you the most?
6. What was your favorite movie monster?
7. If you want to scare somebody, what would you do?
8. Some say that the White House is haunted. If you were a White House ghost, what would you do?
9. What is the best Halloween costume you've ever worn or seen?
10. Franklin D. Roosevelt said, "The only thing we have to fear is fear itself." What do you think about this?
11. Have you ever visited one of those "haunted houses" in an amusement park or neighbor's house? What was it like?
12. What was your worst nightmare?
13. What are people doing in your neighborhood or office for Halloween?

Trick or Treat!

More spine-tingling questions for Halloween or other spooky occasions.

1. What was the worst thing you ever got in your Halloween trick-or-treat bag?
2. What is your favorite Halloween candy?
3. How old is too old for a child to go trick-or-treating?
4. Where is your favorite place to go trick-or-treating?
5. If you could be any monster (such as Dracula, Frankenstein, or a werewolf) what would you be and why?
6. If you were a kid again, what costume would you wear to go trick-or-treating?
7. What was the biggest scare you ever had?
8. What is your favorite thing to do on "a dark and stormy night"?
9. Tell us about a real-life place that is supposed to be haunted.
10. What is your favorite thing about fall?
11. Suppose you became a ghost after you died. What would you do?
12. On camping trips, some people like to tell ghost stories around the campfire. Tell us about your favorite ghost story. Or, tell us about your favorite camping trip.
13. Halloween is the start of the "indulging season" that runs through Thanksgiving and the December holidays. How do you plan to keep from overeating, or are you just planning to enjoy yourself?
14. What was the biggest Halloween trick you ever pulled on someone or someone pulled on you?
15. Tell us about something that grosses you out.
16. Give us a strategy for getting the maximum amount of candy while trick-or-treating.
17. Who is your favorite writer of horror stories?

Holiday Shopping

A perfect set of table topics for holiday shopping season, such as December for Christmas and Hanukkah, or other gift-giving holidays.

1. Who is the hardest person to shop for on your holiday list?
2. What do you think will be the hottest toy this season and why?
3. What would you like as a holiday gift?
4. Another challenge with holiday shopping is hiding your gifts so your spouse/kids/significant others won't see what you bought until you wrap and give them. Where do you hide your gifts?
5. Tell us about your worst experience with holiday shopping.
6. What is your favorite place to shop?
7. One of the most challenging parts of holiday shopping is finding a place to park. What techniques do you use in finding a place to park at a crowded mall?
8. What is the most expensive gift you ever bought?
9. What thing irritates you the most when you go holiday shopping?
10. When do you typically start your holiday shopping? When do you finish?
11. Do you prefer shopping online or in a store? Why?
12. Do you like shopping at malls? Why or why not?
13. You want your spouse or significant other to buy you a special gift. How do you let that person know what you want?
14. How do you deal with a gift that you don't like?

Secret Santa

In the United States, many offices and families have the tradition of the Secret Santa, where people draw the names of coworkers or fellow members from a hat and buy a small gift for that person.

This fun table topics session works the same way. Write the names of the following people on slips of paper. Have each person draw a name and then say what type of gift he or she would buy for that person. If a speaker does not know this person, he or she can discard the name and draw another one (but only once). After a name has been used or discarded, no one else can use it. You can update the list with current celebrities and news figures.

- Your favorite athlete (tell us which one)
- The Pope
- You
- A famous or infamous popstar (tell us which one)
- The president of your country
- Someone you know who could use some holiday cheer
- The homeless man who walks down the street
- Your best friend
- Your boss at work
- A relative or close friend you have not seen for a long time
- Your pet
- A charity you strongly believe in (tell us which one)
- The love of your life
- Your toaster
- Anyone of your choice
- Your children (or what would you would give your children if you had them)
- Your best friend from high school

Thoughts and Feelings Questions

These table topics questions give participants the opportunity to share their deepest thoughts and feelings. You can expect some fascinating and revealing answers, but you can also expect some people to balk at sharing such personal information – especially if they are new to public speaking. If someone feels uncomfortable answering a question, give him or her the option of answering another question or just ask that person to talk about something else.

Personal Values

These questions encourage speakers to talk about their most deeply held values.

1. What matters most to you?
2. What is the most important value that your parents taught you?
3. What value do you think children need to learn the most?
4. Would are you willing to die for?
5. Out of all the ways you spend your time during the week, which activity do you feel gives you the greatest value?
6. Who is your role model?
7. What would you absolutely never forgive?
8. Do you believe that honesty is the best policy? Why or why not?
9. What is the one thing you absolutely cannot do without?
10. What is the greatest sacrifice you've ever made in your life? Was it worth it?
11. There are many things people are willing to do for love. What are you *not* willing to do?
12. What is the most important thing you want to accomplish in your life?
13. What song is your personal anthem?
14. What book has changed your life?
15. Which motto best expresses your outlook on life?
16. If you had six months left to live, how would you spend your time?
17. If you could change one thing about your life, what would it be?
18. When you are feeling sad or disappointed, how do you raise your spirits?

Courage

These questions give participants the opportunity to share their feelings about courage.

1. Have you or someone you know ever been in physical danger? Tell us about it.
2. John F. Kennedy's 1960 book *Profiles in Courage* was about politicians who showed their courage by standing up for their convictions. Do you think there are any courageous politicians today? If so, who are they?
3. Suppose you are the Wizard of Oz. The Cowardly Lion came to you and asked for courage. What would you give him to make him feel truly brave?
4. Who do you think is braver, men or women?
5. What was the bravest thing you've ever done?
6. Even experienced Toastmasters find themselves getting nervous before an important speech. What encouragement would you give someone before they get up to speak?
7. The major Hollywood studios have gathered together and asked you to come up with the perfect movie hero. Tell us what characteristics such a hero would have.
8. Tell us about someone whose bravery you admire. It could be a relative, someone you know, or someone from history.
9. If someone walked away from a hopeless situation, would you consider that person courageous? Why or why not?
10. Was there ever a time that your courage failed you? Tell you about it.
11. What do you do to build up your courage when you are afraid?
12. There's a thin line that separates bravery from plain ol' irresponsible foolhardiness. So, what was the most foolhardy thing you've ever done?
13. Sometimes, the most courageous thing people can do is to admit they're wrong. Tell us about a situation when you had to admit you were wrong.
14. War gives people many opportunities to show their courage. Tell us who you think was history's most courageous war hero.

Turning Points

We all have moments when our lives go in a different direction. We make a decision or are forced to adapt to changing circumstances – and our lives are never the same. These questions challenge you to talk about these situations. If you don't feel comfortable talking about a situation you faced, you can talk about someone else.

1. When did you choose your career and why?
2. What made you decide to move to the community you live in now?
3. Have you ever been in a situation where you've said to yourself, "I've had enough! I can't take this anymore!" What happened and what did you do next?
4. What was the lowest point in your life? What did you do to deal with it?
5. Have you ever looked forward to something, but you are disappointed when you get it? What did you do?
6. Suppose you were able to change one event in your life. What would you change and how would your life turn out differently?
7. A friend of yours is considering leaving his or her career and starting a new one. What advice would you give?
8. At what point in your life would you retire?
9. Have you ever changed your hairstyle or the type of clothes you wear? Tell us about it and why you made the change.
10. Tell us about a point in your life when you said, "This is who I am, and this is what I'm meant to be."
11. What was your biggest dream as a child, and when did you realize that you could never make it come true?
12. If your life were made into a movie, what would be the major plot twist?
13. Suppose you never left your hometown. How would your life be different?
14. Tell us about a book, movie, or TV show that changed your life.
15. What advice would you give to people who are trying to find their life's purpose?

That Makes Me So Mad!

We try to keep our anger under control, especially in the workplace. Some situations are so extreme, we find ourselves unable to keep our feelings inside. Or can we? By examining the button-pushing situations described in these questions, we may find ways to deal with them.

1. You get a call from your child's principal telling you that he or she got in trouble in school and will be suspended from school. How will you deal with your child when you get home?
2. Which celebrity angers you the most?
3. You came up with a great idea at work and shared it with your boss. You then find out that your boss is promoting your idea, but he is claiming it as his own. How do you respond?
4. What situation would cause you to use profanity?
5. How do you deal with a rude customer?
6. What is your spouse's or partner's most irritating habit?
7. Tell us about a time you were offended by something someone said. How did you deal with it?
8. Whether we call it "cutting in line" or "jumping queues," no one likes it when someone sneaks ahead of us in line. How do you deal with that situation?
9. Has someone ever made you so angry that you wanted to punch that person in the face?
10. How do you calm yourself down when you are very angry?
11. What social or political issue upsets you the most?
12. You're sitting next to the screaming baby on the airplane. What do you do?
13. You get to the register at your favorite fast food restaurant, and the person behind the register seems rude and inattentive. How do you deal with this?
14. Some experts say having regular arguments helps build better relationships. Do you agree with this? Why or why not?
15. How do you react when someone says something really stupid?

Opposing View

Learning how to argue an opposing view from yours enables you to do the following:
- *Identify weaknesses in your argument.*
- *Understand your opponent's objections to your point of view so that you can address them.*
- *Show knowledge and respect for opposing view so that you can earn the respect and attention of your audience.*

Follow these rules for table topics:
- *A participant chooses the number of a question.*
- *Participants must give* convincing *arguments. They also should not cheat by saying they support the opposing view so that they can give a convincing argument for their side.*
- *Ask the audience to vote for the person who gave the most* convincing *argument.*

1. Tell us why your leading competitor's product is better than yours.
2. Tell us why insults, shouting, and vulgar language are important parts of effective communications.
3. Which celebrity do you despise the most? Tell us what you admire the most about this person.
4. Pretend you are your biggest enemy. Why does that person dislike you so much?
5. What is your favorite hobby? Why is it a big waste of time?
6. What is your greatest dream in life? Imagine that a friend or relative is trying to talk you out of pursuing that dream. What would that person say?
7. What is your career? How would you talk a young person out of pursuing a career like yours?
8. What do you think is the worst show on TV? Convince us to watch it.
9. Who is your favorite author, movie star, or athlete? Why do you dislike this person?
10. What is your most prized possession? Why are you sorry you bought it?
11. Tell us why you feel good manners are pretentious and unnecessary.
12. Why would living in some other city be better than living in your own city?

Get Happy!

What does happiness mean to you?

1. How do you reward yourself when you've finished a large project?
2. What makes you laugh?
3. Some people get happy when they enjoy their favorite food. What's yours?
4. What picks up your spirits after a rough day at work?
5. What was the happiest moment of your life?
6. Schadenfruede is happiness at the misfortune of others. What type of misfortune would make you feel happy and why?
7. Who makes you the happiest?
8. Do you feel you can be happy by yourself or do you need to be with other people?
9. Everyone has a happy place. What's yours?
10. Do you feel that every movie needs a happy ending? Why or why not?
11. What song puts you in a cheerful mood?
12. How would you cheer up someone who is sad?
13. Who do you trust more, people in a good mood or a bad mood? Why?
14. Disneyland is called "The Happiest Place on Earth." Do you think that's true?
15. They wish you "Happy Birthday," but do you think birthdays are really happy?
16. What trait do you feel is necessary for happiness?

What Do You Think Of...

What do you think of the following things?

1. ...When you see two people arguing?
2. ...When you see a beautiful sunset?
3. ...When you see a homeless person walk down the street?
4. ...When you see your country's flag?
5. ...When someone gets mad at you?
6. ...When you hear a dirty joke?
7. ...When you are happy?
8. ...When someone passes gas?
9. ...When someone insults you?
10. ...When you see your spouse when you come home from work?
11. ...When you see someone shoplift?
12. ...When you lose a game?
13. ...When you eat your favorite food?
14. ...When you see someone talking to herself?
15. ...When you see children playing?
16. ...When you are trying to assemble a toy for your child, and it breaks.
17. ...When you are grocery shopping, and the thing you need the most is out of stock.
18. ...When you are alone?
19. ...When there is nothing good to watch on TV?
20. ...When you are in the shower?

Life Stages

These questions ask people to share experiences and feelings about different stages of their lives.

1. What is your earliest memory?
2. What was your favorite childhood experience?
3. What was your happiest age and why?
4. What was the hardest part of being a teenager?
5. Do you think people should attend their high school reunions? Why or why not?
6. At what age do you think a person can truly consider himself or herself an adult?
7. How did you celebrate your 18th birthday?
8. At what age did you stop considering yourself young (or do you still consider yourself young)?
9. George Bernard Shaw said, "Youth is wasted on the young." Do you agree?
10. Tell us about the hardest time of your life.
11. Victor Hugo said, "Forty is the old age of youth; fifty the youth of old age." What do you think about this statement?
12. What do you think is better, energy or wisdom?
13. When do you think someone can truly be considered old?
14. If you could choose, how long would you like to live?

What Do You Do?

Tell what decision you would make in each of the following situations and why.

1. You find a five dollar bill in the parking lot of a supermarket. No one is around. There isn't a car nearby.
2. You are shopping where they give out free food samples. You arrive at a table where there is one cheesecake sample left. Then, an older woman arrives, and then a six-year-old girl. Both of them are eyeing that last sample.
3. There are only three days left until the deadline for completing your software project, there is a major feature you have to finish. You can slap together some code that may be buggy and will be difficult to update later on, but you will finish on time. If you took the time to write the code correctly, it would take an extra week.
4. A friend asks you to watch her apartment while she is on a business trip. While you are there, you accidentally break one of her favorite coffee mugs.
5. A coworker keeps nagging you to buy some wrapping paper from her daughter's school fundraiser. There isn't a single roll of wrapping paper that you would want to buy.
6. You are the company's accountant. You find some irregularities in your boss's expense reports.
7. Your eight-year-old passes gas in the middle of a religious service.
8. You and your family are trying to enjoy a meal at a nice restaurant. The lady in the table next to yours has been talking on her cell phone for the past fifteen minutes – and talking about personal things you don't want your children to hear.
9. You're supposed to drive home after the office party. An already tipsy coworker is pushing you to have an apple martini and won't leave you alone until you do.
10. You're in line at the customer service department waiting to return some merchandise. The man in front of you is trying to return an item without a receipt and is arguing with the clerk because she can't accept it.
11. You have to go to the bathroom. The person has been in the only stall for the past ten minutes.
12. A stranger asks if he can borrow your cell phone. He explains that his car broke down, but you don't see a broken down car nearby.

Making Changes

Change is scary, but it is often necessary. These questions enable you to share your feelings and experiences with change.

1. Why is change necessary for growth?
2. Tell us about something you had to give up in order for you to have the life you have now.
3. For most people, adolescence is a time of rapid and difficult change. What changes did you make as a teenager and how did they shape you?
4. What was the most difficult change you ever had to make in your life?
5. Do you think people should move away from the place where they grew up? Why or why not?
6. Tell us about a change you made that you wound up regretting.
7. Can changing your hair or clothing style really change your outlook? Why or why not?
8. What advice would you give to someone who is thinking about getting a divorce?
9. What was the biggest but easiest change you ever had to make?
10. Do you think people should change their habits to address threats to the global environment? Why or why not?
11. How has getting older changed you?
12. What part of your life or yourself would you absolutely refuse to change?
13. Tell us about a change you would like to make sometime in the future?
14. What change would you be willing to make to improve your life?
15. How do you think your life will change in the next five years?

Big Issues

Political issues come and go, but these questions delve into the overriding values behind your views. Get ready for some thought-provoking questions and eye-opening answers.

1. What obligation, if any, do you think rich people have to the poor in society?
2. Do you think powerful countries should intervene in conflicts between smaller countries?
3. When people are subject to oppression, how do you feel they should respond?
4. Should there be laws to prevent people from engaging in self-destructive behavior, such as alcohol and drug use?
5. Do you feel people are inherently selfish or altruistic? How does this shape your political views?
6. If another country is acting aggressively towards its neighbors or groups within its borders, how do you think your country should respond?
7. What type of regulations and restrictions, if any, should be placed on businesses operating in your country?
8. Do you feel that media should be limited in some way to prevent content from reaching those who might be offended by it?
9. What should society do about non-conformists and others whose viewpoints, lifestyles, and art are different from the majority?
10. Every society has children, elderly, and physically or mentally impaired who can't take care of themselves. What, if anything, should society do for them?
11. What is the maximum you would pay in taxes?
12. What role, if any, should government have in education?
13. Should a society have a standard of moral conduct that everyone must follow?
14. What society, real or imaginary, do you think is or was the closest to utopia?
15. What do you feel society should do to those who violate the law?

Potpourri Questions

This section contains questions with a variety of themes. You will find something that fits your group.

Finish This

The following are the openings for table topics. Each speaker has to fill in the supporting points and conclusion.

1. The main way that Toastmasters has benefited me is...
2. Let me tell you about the most embarrassing moment I've had with my friends. It happened the other day when...
3. It was a terrible feeling when I said something that embarrassed or offended someone. I realized something was wrong when...
4. I won $26 million in the lottery? Wow! That's a lot of money. Here is how I will spend it...
5. There was a time in my life when I felt a great deal of disappointment and felt like giving up. Here is what I faced and how I overcame it...
6. Tonight, I feel like the happiest person in the world! And I feel so happy because ...
7. You're taking me to my favorite restaurant, and I can have anything on the menu? Well, where I want to go and what I want to eat is...
8. I usually don't splurge on luxuries. But, when I saw this, I knew I had to have it and the heck with the price. Let me tell you what I bought...
9. There are two things that I believe are essential for success. The first is...
10. I suppose all of us have a "guilty pleasure," such as a reading trashy romance novels or indulging in a triple-scoop hot-fudge sundae. My guilty pleasure is...
11. I begin every morning by following a certain daily ritual. When I first get out of bed, I...
12. Whenever I have a bad day or generally feeling down, I can always count on this to help me feel better. The thing that lifts my spirits the most is...
13. I suppose that everybody excelled in one thing or another when they're in high school. The thing I did the best in high school was...
14. I'm really looking forward to summer. Aren't you? Here are things I plan to do...
15. When I first came to Toastmasters, I felt a bit nervous because I was in unfamiliar surroundings and had to do something that terrified me: speak in public. What finally made me feel comfortable and gave me the confidence to speak was this...

16. I'm usually a very tolerant person, but when people have this one annoying habit – Argggh! – I just can't stand it! This habit that irritates me the most is…
17. I would like to thank the Academy for this prestigious award. I'd like to thank…

The Language of Flowers

American Girl *magazine had an article about how people in the Victorian era assigned meanings to each type of flower and plant. Girls put together small flower arrangements called* tussie-mussies *that have messages based on the flowers selected.*

For these table topics, have the participant pick a flower. Then, you give its definition and a question based on that definition.

- Azalea – First love: Tell us about your first love.
- Daffodil – Respect: Tell us about a friend, family member, or acquaintance who you especially respect.
- Fern – Fascination: What fascinates you?
- Geranium – Comfort: What is the most comfortable outfit you wear?
- Lavender – Good luck: Do you believe in luck?
- Mums – Cheerfulness: Do you consider people who are cheerful pleasant or annoying?
- Parsley – Thanks: Parsley is the plant of thanks, and yet, restaurants use it as a garnish that we throw away. What do you think about this?
- Red rose – Love: How would you define love?
- Rosemary – Remembrance: Tell us about a special person in your life who is no longer living.
- Sage – Wisdom: Wisdom usually comes from experience. Tell us about an experience in your life that made you wiser.
- Tulip – Fame: Would you want to be famous? Why or why not?
- Yellow Rose – Friendship: Who is your best friend and why?

Dogs

Questions about dogs (even for those who are not canine lovers).

1. What do you think is the hardest part of owning a dog?
2. What is your favorite dog in the movies, television, or comic strips?
3. They say that dogs are man's best friend. Do you agree? Why or why not?
4. They say "a dog's bark is worse than its bite." Do you also think that's true about people?
5. The first dogs were domesticated hundreds of thousands of years ago. Tell us how you think that might have happened.
6. What do you think are better, dogs or cats? Why?
7. Do you think that dog racing should be made illegal? Why or why not?
8. Tell us about your most vivid memory involving dogs when you were growing up. It could be about your dog or someone else's.
9. What advice would you to give to someone who wants to get a dog?
10. Were you afraid of dogs when you were a child? Why or why not?
11. Some women say, "All men are dogs." Tell us your opinion about this.
12. What do you think is the proper way to discipline a dog?
13. Tell us about your *least* favorite breed of dog.
14. Why do dogs look like their owners?

Cats

We can't have dog questions without cat questions. Tell us your feelings about felines.

1. Why are cat videos so popular on the Internet?
2. What do you think is the hardest part of owning a cat?
3. What is your favorite cat in the movies, television, or comic strips?
4. Tell us about your most vivid memory involving cats when you were growing up. It could be about your cat or someone else's.
5. Why do you think people consider cats to be evil?
6. How do you get a cat to stop scratching the drapes and furniture?
7. Jean Cocteau said, "I love cats because I enjoy my home; and little by little, they become its visible soul." What do you think about this statement?
8. What advice would you to give to someone who wants to get a cat?
9. What famous cat most resembles you?
10. They say, "Curiosity killed the cat." Is curiosity always that dangerous?
11. Why are cats so cute?
12. What do you think is happier being with humans, cats or dogs?
13. Why do some people hate cats?
14. Ancient Egyptians worshipped cats as gods. Do you think we still worship cats today?

How Do I?

All of us give instructions every day. In the office, we tell people how to do tasks. We tell friends how to drive to our house, or tell a hairstylist how we want our hair cut. By learning how to give clear instructions, we can make sure the job is done right.

Have the participants pick a number and give instructions for that particular task. They can give straightforward directions or be funny and imaginative. If they don't know how to do something, they can make something up. The key is to be clear and logical.

1. How do I...mow a lawn?
2. How do I...eat an artichoke?
3. How do I...watch movies from a streaming video service?
4. How do I...make a friend?
5. How do I...lose weight?
6. How do I...use a toaster?
7. How do I...play checkers (draughts)?
8. How do I...build a house?
9. How do I...take a photograph?
10. How do I...deal with mean people?
11. How do I...bake a cake?
12. How do I...be happy?
13. How do I...play golf?
14. How do I...spread a computer virus?
15. How do I...eat corn on the cob?
16. How do I...give a speech?
17. How do I...ride a bicycle?
18. How do I...use a fork?
19. How do I...use social media?
20. How do I...drive a car?

#masteringtabletopics Questions

If you follow me on Twitter (@maswriter), you can get a daily table topics question with the hashtag #masteringtabletopics. Here is a collection of questions I posted on Twitter.

1. What do you think is your best quality?
2. What was the most embarrassing thing that ever happened to you at work?
3. What scientific achievement do you hope to see in your lifetime?
4. Why are books about undead characters such as vampires, zombies, and ghosts so popular?
5. What time of day do you feel the most productive and why?
6. What advice would you give someone who thinks nobody likes him or her?
7. Have you ever gotten angry because your favorite performer didn't win on an awards show? Why?
8. Did you ever make a prediction that turned out to be true? Tell us about it.
9. Tell us about a championship or other competition that you won.
10. What modern-day hero deserves a movie about his or her life?
11. Why do you feel some businesses are more successful than others?
12. When you have a deadline, do you prefer doing the task as soon as possible or waiting for the last possible minute?
13. Which store, restaurant, or other business from your past do you wish was still around today?
14. With the flood of information we get on a daily basis, how do you pick the bits that are important?
15. Tell us about a speech that caused you to vote for or against a candidate.
16. What holiday custom celebrated in another country do you wish was celebrated in yours?
17. Tell us about a time when you had to think outside of the box.

Let's Go to the Movies!

Who doesn't love the movies? These questions get you thinking about movies you've seen (whether in theaters, on TV, or streaming) and imagining movies you would make yourself.

1. What type of movie would you absolutely refuse to see?
2. What is your favorite place to sit in a movie theater?
3. Suppose you made a sequel of your most favorite movie. Which movie is it and what is the plot?
4. Where do you prefer watching movies, at home or in a theater? Why?
5. What was the worst movie you've ever seen?
6. If you were to make a movie of your life, what type of movie would it be and who would star in it?
7. You're creating a remake of a movie from the past. Which movie is it and how would you change it?
8. Which do you think are better, movies today or movies 25 years ago?
9. Who is your favorite movie star?
10. What book do you think should be made into a movie?
11. What movie or performance do you feel most deserved an Academy Award?
12. Tell us about your favorite "guilty pleasure" movie.
13. Do you feel that Hollywood has run out of ideas for movies?
14. Some say that popular movies are a reflection of society. What do you think today's movies say about our times?
15. Tell us about a movie you've seen more than once.
16. What is your favorite movie-time snack?

Think Fast!

Table topics about situations when you have to think quickly.

1. You are walking through a less-than-safe part of town. A man is walking towards you, but you can't see him very well. What do you do?
2. Your house is on fire. After you got everyone in your family to safety, what personal belonging would you try to save?
3. You are pulled over by a police officer. He says you are speeding when you know you are not. How do you deal with the situation?
4. You get into a car accident, and you're not sure who is at fault. What do you do?
5. The keynote speaker for a professional conference you are attending just got stuck at the airport. The conference organizers ask you to speak in that person's place – in front of 1,000 of your peers – and you have to go on in five minutes. What do you do? If you speak, what do you speak about?
6. You are visiting another country with a tour group and got separated from your traveling companions. You find yourself stuck in a village where no one speaks your language. What do you do?
7. You are with your family at the company picnic. Your company president comes over to visit you – just as your kids have become hot, bored, and tired enough to start acting up. What do you do?
8. You have been kidnapped. What do you do?
9. You are traveling in another city when you lose your wallet, along with your money, credit cards, and ID.
10. At your family's reunion picnic, two of your relatives start a fight over a disagreement that happened years ago. The relatives start bringing other people onto their sides, and the dispute spreads through the whole group. What do you do?
11. You have ten minutes to get to your gate at the airport, and you're stuck in the security line. What do you do?
12. It's 4:00 P.M. You have to pick up your daughter to get her to band rehearsal at 4:20, and your son to get to his Little League game at 4:30. Then, your boss comes in and says she has a project that must get done before you leave.

Fear Factor

Fear Factor *was a reality game show where contestants performed dangerous and humiliating stunts to win $50,000. We don't have to be on a reality show to come across scary situations. We face scary situations every day, which are covered in these questions.*

1. You want to ask your boss for a raise.
2. Tell us about the first time you spoke in front of an audience.
3. You're eight years old. The schoolyard bully demands that you give him your lunch money or get a pounding.
4. Your doctor wants you to schedule an immediate appointment because she is "concerned" about something in your test results.
5. A robber sticks a gun in your face and demands your money.
6. You're 16. You're parents told you to be home by ten o'clock. It's now one in the morning.
7. You disagree with your boss.
8. You're on an airplane. The man seated next to you seems to be acting jittery and erratic.
9. You're meeting your fiancée's parents for the first time.
10. Your best friend comes from a different culture and invites you to a family dinner of traditional foods. There are some dishes you can't identify and some that look too gross to eat.
11. You're not quite sure how your friend convinced you go skydiving, but you now find yourself standing by the door of the plane, and the instructor orders you to jump.
12. One of your coworkers is making inappropriate advances towards you.
13. You have to climb up into a tall tree to rescue your kid's kite.
14. You're entertaining important guests at a five-star restaurant. When you pay the $300 bill, the waiter tells you that your credit card was declined.
15. Your four-year-old asks you, "Where do babies come from?"

What If?

How would the world be different if some of the events in history had different outcomes? These table topic questions give participants the opportunity to show their knowledge of history and stretch their imagination.

You can give participants a choice of "history buff" questions (for those who are knowledgeable about history) or "non-history buff" questions (written for those who are not into history).

History Buff Questions

1. We all know that if the British defeated George Washington in 1776, there wouldn't be a United States. How do you think the *rest of the world* would have been different?

2. During World War I, British Army Private Henry Tandey saw a wounded German soldier. Tandey later explained, "I took aim but couldn't shoot a wounded man, so I let him go." The soldier he spared was Adolf Hitler. How would the world have been different if Private Tandey didn't spare him?

3. In 1452, Johannes Gutenberg borrowed money so that he could continue his project in printing the Bible with movable type. What do you think would have happened if he couldn't get the money to invent his printing press?

4. Around the year 1000, Viking sailors settled briefly in Newfoundland, becoming the first Europeans to arrive in the Americas. Suppose they were able to settle permanently and build colonies. How would the world be different?

5. The 1844 Potato Famine caused thousands of Irish to leave Ireland for America and other countries. How would the world have been different if the Potato Famine didn't happen?

6. Even after the sinking of the *Luisitania* in 1915, there was still pressure to keep the United States from getting involved in World War I. What do you think would have happened if the United States never entered World War I?

7. Suppose that in 1588, the Spanish Armada defeated the English fleet and conquered England. How do you think the world would be different?

8. What do you think your life would have been like if you lived 1,000 years ago?

9. If you could change the outcome of one historic event of the past 1,000 years, what would it be and why?

Non-History Buff Questions

1. Nineteenth and early twentieth century scientists and inventors like Farraday, Ampere, Edison, and Tesla harnessed electricity and made possible all the electrical gadgets we depend on today. What do you think the world would be like today if we didn't have electricity?
2. The 1904 World's Fair in St. Louis introduced the world to hot dogs and ice cream. What other foods are you glad that were invented?
3. In 1928, Philo T. Farnsworth demonstrated the first electrical television set. How do you think your life would be different if television was never invented?
4. In the eighteenth century, the American colonies switched from the Julian to the Gregorian calendar, which added 11 days to our dates. What would do if you had an extra 11 days?
5. Around 1500, Peter Henlein, a craftsman from Nuremberg, Germany, created the first watch by enclosing a timekeeping movement in a round portable case. How would your life be different if you didn't have to depend on a watch?
6. In 1969, development of the Internet began. How do you think people 100 years from now will regard the creation of the Internet?
7. What do you think was the most important invention in history? What do you think the world would have been like without it?
8. In 1924, Ralph Smedley started the first Toastmasters club, which continues to meet to this day in Tustin, California. How would your life be different if Toastmasters wasn't invented?

Free Advice

One of the "table topics" we run into in our daily lives is when someone asks us for advice. For this exercise, have the participant pretend that a friend or coworker asking for advice on a subject.

1. How do you pick a good dentist?
2. I need to buy a new computer for my home. Which one should I get?
3. I want to take my family on a nice trip. We want to get out of town, but we don't want to go too far out of the area. Where do you recommend we go?
4. I am having trouble going to sleep at night. What do you recommend I do?
5. Help! I have only 24 hours to scrape up $1,500 for the rent, or I'll be evicted! What should I do!!
6. I am trying to lose weight. I've tried all the diets, but they don't seem to work for me. What do you suggest I do?
7. I just inherited $10,000 from my dear sainted Aunt Hildragard. What should I do with it?
8. I can't get my two-year-old to eat good food. He won't touch his vegetables and meat. All he wants is ice cream. What do I do?
9. We are running out of space in our house. We could either add on to our existing house or buy a bigger one. What do you suggest we do?
10. My company needs to get a new accounting software system. How do we go about choosing the right system for us?
11. My brother is down on his luck. He lost his job, he had his car repossessed, and now he lives with us. My wife and I love my brother very much, but having him live with us is getting pretty old. How do we help him get back on his feet?
12. I was just promoted to supervisor. Now, I have to hire a new staff member for the department. I've never hired anyone before. How do I go about picking the right person?
13. What can I do to put the spark back into my marriage?
14. My 18-year-old daughter is leaving home for the first time to go to college. What advice should I give her?

Why?

Why ask these table topics questions? Because they are fun and interesting.

1. Why do you think people tend to overeat during the holidays?
2. Why did you join Toastmasters?
3. Why does a bottle of wine cost twice as much in a restaurant than it does in a supermarket?
4. Why do so many people fantasize about becoming a best-selling author but never try to write a book?
5. Why do you care?
6. Why does gasoline cost more in one city than another?
7. Why do fools fall in love?
8. Why do people tend to focus on what's wrong with their lives instead of what's right?
9. Why in movies do they often make the villain more interesting than the hero?
10. Why are words that describe waste elimination and reproduction – two bodily functions necessary for human survival – considered obscene?
11. Why are you here?
12. Why can a person forget to pick up a loaf of bread at the store but still remember a grudge he's been holding for decades?
13. Why do we call these "table topics" when you have to leave your seat at the table to answer them?
14. Why do people wait until the last minute to buy gifts?
15. Why do people make New Year's resolutions and never keep them?
16. Why haven't we gone back to the moon since the early 1970's?
17. Why do people fear public speaking more than death?
18. Why has practically every popular musician put out a Christmas album?
19. Why do people feel they have to visit family during the holidays?
20. Why do the most worthwhile things in life require the most effort?

Eighties Retro

Did you grow up in the 1980s? Here is an opportunity to relive the days of big hair and shoulder pads.

1. Tell us about an article of clothing you wore in the 1980s that you would now be embarrassed to admit you wore.
2. The 1980s were the beginning of the music video business. What was your favorite music video from that time?
3. Where were you when the space shuttle *Challenger* exploded?
4. Where did you live in the 1980s?
5. The personal computer business boomed in the 1980s with an increasing number of people using computers for the first time. Tell us about the first computer you ever used.
6. If we're into eighties retro now, we can imagine that one day, there will be retro from this decade. Which fads and music from this decade do you think will be revived in the future?
7. Which fashions from the 1980s do you hope *will* come back into vogue in this decade?
8. Several times in the 1980s, musicians gathered together to sing for charity. This included Band Aid, USA for Africa, and Farm Aid. Which charity would you like to see musicians gather together and sing for today?
9. Were the 1980s a good time for you?
10. How would you explain the 1980s to someone who wasn't born until after that time?
11. Who do you think was the worst musician or musical group in the 1980s?
12. The 1980s marked the end of the Cold War and the fall of the Iron Curtain. Share your memories of that time.
13. The hit TV series *Hill Street Blues* always began with the catchphrase, "Let's be careful out there." What catchphrase do you use to start your day?
14. If you could go back in time and relive an event from the 1980s, which one would it be and why?

The Last Forty Years

Forty is an age of reflection. Whether you've reached and past that age or if it is still a few years away, here are some questions to get you to reflect on change and growth over time.

1. What do you think is the greatest change in the past forty years?
2. If you can go back forty years and bring back one souvenir to sell on eBay, what would it be?
3. What is your favorite musician of the past forty years?
4. What technology developed in the past forty years can you not live without?
5. What do you think has gotten worse in the last forty years?
6. Do you consider yourself the same person at forty as you were when you were twenty?
7. Do you think children today have a better life than you did forty years ago?
8. What do you think the world will be like forty years from now?
9. What advice would you give to someone who is turning forty?
10. Tell us about an important historic event that happened during your childhood. What do you remember about it?
11. Why do some forty-year-olds go through a mid-life crisis?
12. How did turning forty make you feel?
13. What age are you looking forward to?
14. How will you celebrate your next milestone birthday?

A Mile in Your Shoes

The old saying goes, "Don't judge people until you've walked a mile in their shoes." For these questions, describe what type of person you would be if you wore one of these types of shoes.

1. Sandy army boots
2. Basketball shoes
3. Sandals
4. Skateboard shoes
5. No shoes
6. Clown shoes (red size 42 DDD)
7. Wooden clogs
8. Hiking boots
9. No-name brand slightly irregular running shoes
10. Flip-flops (with socks)
11. Steel-toed work boots
12. Black wingtips
13. Plastic bags
14. Ballet slippers
15. Jester shoes (green with curled up toes and bells)
16. Two-tone designer pumps with four-inch heels
17. Ice skating boots with toe picks
18. Bunny slippers
19. Saddle shoes with black patent leather
20. Hand-tooled leather cowboy boots

Speech Contest Questions

The following questions have been collected from Toastmasters speech contests. Use them for your contests.

1. If you suddenly found the courage to do one thing you've always wanted to do, what would it be?
2. If you had to change careers, what would your new career be?
3. If you had one question that you could ask every adult, and they had to answer it honestly, what would that question be and why?
4. Education is the foundation of our formative years. Tell us about a particular event in your school years and what made it so important.
5. Suppose you are trick or treating on Halloween. What would you do if someone didn't give you a treat?
6. Which one of the five senses – hearing, smell, feeling, taste, or sight – is the most important to you and why.
7. What do you think is the greatest problem facing humanity today? What can you *personally* do about it?
8. What is the most valuable thing you've gained from Toastmasters?
9. How do you think the world will change in 100 years?
10. Why is failure an often necessary ingredient of success?
11. If an alien from another planet whisked you onto its spaceship and asked you to explain the human race to its people, what would you say?
12. You are given a box that contains the one thing you've always wanted in life. What is in the box? Would you open it?

Other Ideas for Table Topics

Questions are not the only prompts you can use for table topics. Here are some other ways that you can run a table topics session.

- Buy a bag of fortune cookies. Have each person open a cookie, read the fortune inside, and then give a speech about it.

- Start a story circle. As topicmaster, give a brief beginning of a story. Then, ask another person to continue the story. Use the regular table topic timing. When one person finishes, ask someone else to continue the story.

- Cut out pictures from magazines and mount them on cardboard. Ask someone to take a picture and describe what describe what happened.

- Put some small household items in a bag. The more unusual, the better. Each person reaches into the bag, takes an item, and then tells the audience why they should buy the item.

- Cut out newspaper headlines. Look for especially unusual or intriguing ones. Have each person make up a story that goes with the headline.

- Here's the pitch: Have everyone give a one-minute pitch for a product, which could be one they sell or one they make up. Have the audience vote on who gave the most convincing pitch.

Your possibilities for table topics are limitless! Try these or make up some of your own.

How to Develop Your Own Questions

After you have given a few of these table topic questions, you can start developing your own. Writing table topic questions is a speaking exercise in itself. By learning how to ask good questions, you can encourage useful responses from others.

Here are some tips to help you write table topic questions:

- Build your questions around a theme. This stimulates your creativity. As you think of a question that fits your theme, others will flow forth. This also helps participants prepare for the questions they receive.

- Make your questions open-ended, which means that they require an explanation instead of a simple yes or no. If you give a close-ended, yes or no question, ask for an explanation or details. For example, "If someone served you food you didn't like, would you eat it anyway? Why or why not?"

- Keep your questions simple. Only provide details that are necessary for answering the question.

- Ask only one main question per table topic. Avoid stringing together unrelated questions, such as "Where do you like to go on vacation? Do you find work too stressful?" This frustrates speakers because they do not know what question to answer first, and they may find it difficult to fit a complete response in the allotted time. You can combine related questions, such as "Where do you like to go on vacation? What do you like to do when you get there?"

- Avoid leading questions that push speakers to respond one way, such as "Do think the barbaric slaughter of innocent animals for food is morally wrong?" This question forces the participant to answer one way and doesn't permit an opposing view.

Additional Resources

This section lists books, games, and apps that are available for developing your table topics skills. This listing does not imply endorsement, and no promotional consideration was given for these products to be included. Check the product descriptions at the indicated links and see product reviews. Product reviews and information about new products will be available at: http://www.matthewarnoldstern.com/tabletopics.html.

Books and Games

The Book of Questions Series

The Book of Questions series is available at most bookstores or from Workman Publishing (http://www.workman.com).

TableTalk

The TableTalk conversation card set is available from Toastmasters International (http://www.toastmasters.org), catalog number 1318.

TableTopics

The TableTopics line of products offers questions in a variety of subjects with special editions for different occasions. TableTopics is available at retail stores and at the TableTopics website (http://www.tabletopics.com).

Apps for Table Topics

The following apps for smartphones, tablets, and personal computers can help with speech timing and provide additional questions. Refer to the following websites for pricing and information or visit your device's application store.

Timing Apps

- Presentation Clock by Shawn Welch (iPhone/iPad/Android): Customizable timer with large

digits and notification options.
http://anythingsimple.com/project/presentation-clock/

- SpeakerClock by Drobnik, KG (iPhone/iPad): Timer with large digits and programmable indicator lights.
http://www.cocoanetics.com/apps/speakerclock/

- SpeechTime Pro by Indigo Stars (iPhone/iPad): Enables you to define ten customizable presets for different types of speeches. Stores speech durations in a log. Free Lite version also available without customizable presets.
http://speechtimepro.indigostars.net

- Speech Timer by Basil Salad Software (iPhone/iPad/Mac): Features large digits and indicators. Can be use as timing lights in meetings. Exportable speech logs.
http://basilsalad.com/ios/speech-timer/

- Speech Timer by Michael Dobbins (Android): Presets for different types of Toastmasters speeches. Color indicators also have letters for colorblind speakers.
http://www.hellogovernance.com/android-apps

Table Topic Question Apps

- Off the Cuff! by Charabaruk Information Services (Windows Phone): Contains questions on a variety of topics. http://www.windowsphone.com/en-us/store/app/off-the-cuff/b04ed1b4-5623-45b1-95ad-027714aaec86

- TABLETOPICS by Aloompa (iPhone/iPad): Includes questions on a range of topics and additional sets.
https://itunes.apple.com/us/app/tabletopics/id399147630?mt=8

- Table Topics by Joshua McWilliams (Android): Includes a variety of questions and enables you to add your own.
https://play.google.com/store/apps/details?id=com.mcwilliams.TableTopicsApp&hl=en

- Table Topics Plus by Cyberworkz (iPhone/iPad): Offers over 100 ideas for Table Topics sessions organized by theme and skill level.
https://itunes.apple.com/ca/app/table-topics+/id980883932?mt=8

Index

Awards, 5
Background information, 8
Body, 11
Body language, 14
Breadth, 9
Clothing, 14
Conclusion, 12
Cultural differences, 8
Delivery techniques, 12
Depth, 9
Eye contact, 13
Fortune cookies, 89
Gestures, 14
Leading questions, 91
Listening, 7
Open-ended questions, 91
Opening, 11
Organization
    general rule for, 10
    importance of, 10
    quick, 12
    technique, 9
Overtime, 5
Pauses, 13
Pitches, 89
Questions
    apps, 94
    background information in, 8
    clarifying, 8
    creating, 91
    methods of asking, 4
    resources for further, 93
    themes for, 3
    understanding, 7
Speech contests, timing, 5
Story circles, 89
Table topics
    alternatives to questions, 89
    examples, 14
    listening and, 7
    overview, 1
    timing of, 4
    topics to cover in, 9
    voting, 5
Themes, creating questions around, 91
Time indicators, 4
Timekeeper, 4
Timing, 4
Timing apps, 4, 93
Topicmaster, 3
Topics, selecting, 9
Vocal variety, 13
Voting, 5

Made in the USA
Coppell, TX
22 April 2022